Physics Lab in a
Hardware Store

Physics Lab in a Hardware Store

by BOB FRIEDHOFFER

Illustrated by Joe Hosking

FRANKLIN WATTS
A Division of Grolier Publishing

New York • London • Hong Kong • Sydney
Danbury, Connecticut

To Rodney Ezrapour, who always demonstrates
the importance of having a knowledge of center
of gravity, friction, motion, and balance when
riding a dirt bike. Thanks for falling.

Library of Congress Cataloging-in-Publication Data

Friedhoffer, Robert
Physics lab in a hardware store/by Bob Friedhoffer; illustrated by Joe Hosking.
    p.cm. — (Physical science labs)
    Includes bibliographical references and index.
    Summary: Examines such topics in physics as mass, weight, gravity, buoyancy, and pressure with experiments using common household tools.
    ISBN 0-531-11292-6 (lib. bdg.)   ISBN 0-531-15823-3 (pbk.)
    1. Physics—Experiments—Juvenile literature. 2. Scientific recreations—Juvenile literature. 3. Hardware—Juvenile literature. [1. Physics—Experiments. 2. Experiments 3. Tools.] I. Hosking, Joe, ill. II. Title. III. Series.
QC26.F75   1996
621.9'01'53—dc20   96-15828
                                                CIP AC

Acknowledgments

Annette who puts up with my home fix-it-up projects. Richard Crist, ABD (all but dissertation), who uses his tools—books—to come up with the right word or idea. My grandfather, Louis Helfand, who inspired my lifelong love affair with tools. My father, Nat Friedhoffer, who built a nifty workshop in the basement of the homestead on Berkshire Drive. My brother Jeff, who broke things, so I could learn to repair them. The guy who first said, "If it ain't broke, don't fix it!"

Contents

Physics Lab in a Hardware Store

Preface

Browsing through hardware stores can be fun, interesting, and informative. Hardware stores sell tools and supplies used by mechanics, plumbers, carpenters, homeowners, hobbyists, and do-it-yourselfers. When you have—and know how to use—tools, you can demolish, disassemble, fix, or build just about anything.

I was very lucky as a youngster. My grandfather, Louis Helfand, was an expert mechanic and woodworker. He came to live in my parent's house when I was about 10 years old. While he lived with us, he showed me the correct way to use and care for tools. It was through his patience, and his ability to explain the functions of tools, that I became interested in both the tools and the scientific principles that allow them to work.

Grandpa took tools very seri-ously. He praised the ones that were well made and cursed the ones that weren't. In other words, he told it like it was.

When I walk through a hard-ware store today, I remember Grandpa pointing out the tools, both good and bad. Sometimes his comments made me laugh so hard that my stomach hurt.

Hardware stores still hold a fascination for me. There always seem to be new, strange, nifty, cool, wonderful machines, and tools. I can look at them, touch them, examine them, and even buy them.

This book is written as a guidebook to help you learn the scientific principles that make some of the tools displayed in a hardware store work. I hope that after reading this book you will enjoy browsing through hardware stores as much as I do. Who knows? One day we might even meet in one.

A Quick Note to Parents and Educators

Physics Lab in a Housewares Store, a companion volume in this series, demonstrates many of the same principles as this book. That has been done with intent. Many of the students who will be attracted to one of the titles will probably not be attracted to the other, due to traditional gender preferences.

Those that are attracted to both will have the added pleasure of finding out that a workshop and a kitchen have many things in common, and that tools found in one might actually be substituted for those commonly used in the other.

Introduction

Tools have been around for a long time.

Until recently, some scientists believed that the ability to use tools separated humans from the rest of the animal kingdom. Scientists now know that some other animals use tools, too. Chimpanzees, for example, sometimes use sticks to reach food. Every angler fish has a built-in tool—a hairlike filament projecting from its body—that it uses to catch smaller fish. It has recently been discovered that crows are also tool users.

When archaeologists (scientists who study ancient civilizations) are trying to determine if a site was inhabited by ancient humans, they look for tools such as flint knives, grinding stones, arrowheads, and stone hammers. We know that the people living in ancient Egypt, Mesopotamia, Greece, and Mesoamerica all used tools made from rocks and wood.

WHY WE USE TOOLS

Why did ancient human populations use tools? For the same reason that we use them today—to make life easier. A tool gives the person using it a *mechanical advantage*. (Definitions for words in italics can be found in the glossary at the end of this book.) Mechanical advantage is the ratio of the *force* exerted by the tool to the force exerted by the person using the tool. In other words, a tool reduces the amount of force a person must exert to perform a job.

A nut or bolt that can't be loosened with your bare fingers, can be easily loosened by a few twists with a wrench. If you apply 10 pounds (4.5 kg) of *input force* to the end of a wrench, the wrench can exert 20 pounds (9 kg), 30 pounds (13.5 kg), or even more *output force* on a nut or bolt. In other words, a tool can be used to increase or magnify the input force.

A tool can also be used to magnify motion. When a broom is used to sweep a floor, small motions of the hands and arms are amplified at the broom's business end. Obtaining the mechanical advantage offered by a tool involves a trade-off. For a tool to increase output force, the person using that tool must apply the force over a greater distance. When you loosen a nut or bolt without a tool, you twist it between one fin-

ger and your thumb. To loosen a nut or bolt with a wrench, you must move your hand, your wrist, and your arm in a large circle.

Here's another example. Imagine that you are at the loading dock at the back of a hardware store. The average loading dock is about 4 feet (1.2 m) above the store's driveway or parking lot. Loading docks are designed so that the floor of the truck is level with the floor of the loading platform. This makes it easier to load and unload materials.

Suppose that a box weighing 120 pounds (54 kg) is on the ground, just below the loading dock platform. Lifting it would require 120 pounds (54 kg) of force over 4 feet (1.2 m) of *vertical* distance.

Instead of lifting the box, you could place it on a dolly or cart and push it up a plank that extends from the ground to the loading dock floor. In this case, the plank is a kind of tool called an *inclined plane*. It takes less force to push or pull an object up an inclined plane than it takes to lift it straight up, but the distance the object travels is greater.

For the purpose of this example, we will assume that the handcart itself weighs nothing and that the wheels on the dolly eliminate all friction between the box and the plank. If the plank is 24 feet (7.3 m) long, you will have to push the box 6 feet (1.8 m) *horizontally* for every 1 foot (30 cm) that it moves vertically. If you decided to lift the box, you would have to move it only a few inches horizontally.

The mechanical advantage of using the plank as a tool is 6 to 1 (length of plank × distance from the ground to the loading dock floor = mechanical advantage). Thus, the drawback of using the plank is that you will have to move the box six times farther. The benefit is that moving it will require only 20 pounds (9 kg) of input force. That's the trade-off.

You can calculate the input force required by dividing the weight of the box (120 pounds) by the mechanical advantage (6). In other words, 120 pounds ÷ 6 = 20 pounds of input force.

NOTE: Scattered throughout this book you will see a safety symbol. Ask an adult to help you whenever you see this symbol. The symbol indicates that the experiment is a little bit dangerous or difficult. I'd hate to see you get discouraged or hurt while you're learning about science in a hardware store.

CHAPTER ONE

Linear Measurements

Measurements are important to scientists as well as to people using tools from a hardware store.

If you wanted to build a doghouse or a tree house, you would probably begin by asking yourself a few questions: How long should the pieces of wood be? How thick? How wide? How large should the hole for the door be?

Height, length, and width are usually measured with rulers. Most hardware stores sell metal rulers, meter

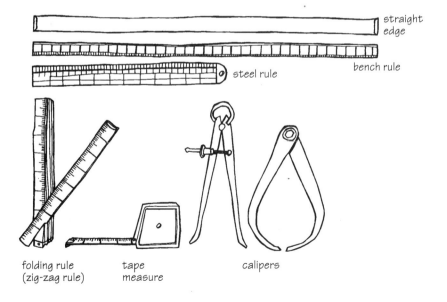

straight edge

bench rule

steel rule

folding rule
(zig-zag rule)

tape
measure

calipers

sticks, yardsticks, tape measures, folding rulers, and calipers. Many of these tools use two measuring systems—metric and English—and have both imprinted on them.

MEASURING SYSTEMS

While the English system is more popular in the United States, the metric system is used in most other countries. Scientists all over the world, even those living in the United States, prefer the metric system. This system uses grams to measure weight, meters to measure length, the Celsius scale to measure temperature, and liters to measure *volume*.

The metric system is generally easier to use because measurements can be converted by simply moving the decimal point. Meters can be converted into centimeters by moving the decimal point two places to the right (0.7 meters = 70 centimeters). Centimeters can be converted into millimeters by moving the decimal point one place to the right (70 cm = 700 mm).

The English system is a little more complicated. There are 12 inches in a foot and 3 feet in a yard. That means that there are 36 inches in a yard ($12 \times 3 = 36$). Therefore, 0.7 yards = 25.2 inches.

Some tools are designed using either the metric system or the English system. Metric wrenches are available in millimeter increments (10 mm, 11 mm, 12 mm). Wrenches based on the English system are available in fractional increments (1/8 inch, 3/16 inch, 1/4 inch, 9/64 inch). In most cases, fractional wrenches fit only fractional nuts and bolts and metric wrenches fit only metric nuts and bolts.

To be a versatile handyperson, you will probably need metric tools as well as English tools. In general, most carpentry tools use the English system. Working on cars, motorcycles, and bicycles may require either English or metric tools, depending on where they were manufactured and which system the designing engineer preferred.

TAPE MEASURES

One of the most common types of rulers found in the hardware store is the tape measure. A tape measure is a ruler on a thin, metal strip. The strip, or tape, is housed inside a metal or plastic case. Most tape measures are small enough to fit in your pocket.

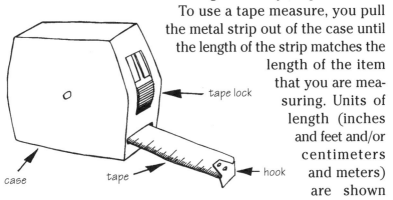

To use a tape measure, you pull the metal strip out of the case until the length of the strip matches the length of the item that you are measuring. Units of length (inches and feet and/or centimeters and meters) are shown on the strip. When you have finished measuring, the strip automatically recoils back into its case. The automatic action is due to a spring that is wound up when the tape is pulled from the case.

CALIPERS

Open-jawed Calipers

Open-jawed calipers consist of two curved legs that are hinged together at the top. The hinge is either a firm joint or a spring joint. The firm-jointed caliper stays open to hold measurements through *friction*, while the spring-jointed caliper holds its measurement by means of an adjusting screw.

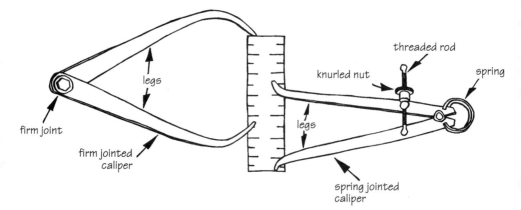

Calipers allow you to measure distances in areas where a ruler does not fit. One type of open-jawed caliper can be used to measure the distance between a surface and the inner dimensions of a drilled or machined hole. A second type can measure the thickness or outer diameter of a material.

To check dimensions, the caliper is adjusted on the piece being measured and then compared to the scale on a ruler. A machinist or carpenter can also adjust the caliper to a specific distance on a scale and then compare the caliper to the work already done. This allows the craftsperson to see how much more cutting, sawing, or filing is necessary to complete the job.

Vernier Calipers

Vernier calipers were introduced in 1631 in a book called *The Construction, Uses, and Properties of a New Mathematica Quadrant.* They are named after their inventor, Pierre Vernier, a French mathematician, inventor, and government official. Vernier calipers are much more precise— and more expensive—than open-jawed calipers because they have a precision measurement scale built in.

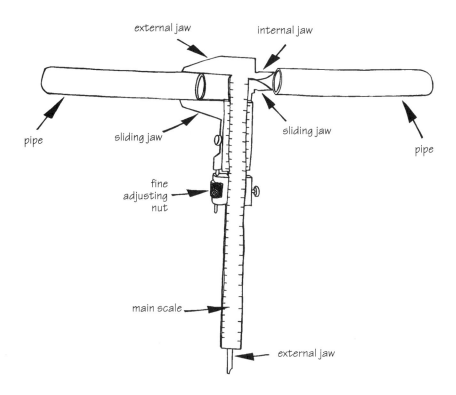

external jaw · internal jaw · pipe · sliding jaw · sliding jaw · pipe · fine adjusting nut · main scale · external jaw

OBSERVATION 1

Use both open-jawed and Vernier calipers to measure the thickness of a nail, an iron pipe, or the handle of a hammer. Which type of caliper is easier to use?

CHAPTER TWO

Friction

Put your hands together, palm to palm, and rub them back and forth vigorously. Did they get warm? If not, something is wrong with you! Have your mom or dad take you to the doctor at once!

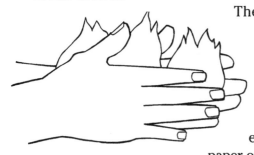

The friction between your two hands, combined with the movement of the two hands, caused the heating. Has a strong gust of wind ever ripped a piece of paper out of your hand? The friction between the paper and the air causes the paper to fly about, rather than just fall to the ground.

Friction is a force that exists between any two surfaces that are in contact with each other. This force resists the motion of the two surfaces. All matter—solids, liquids, and gases—are affected by friction.

EXPERIMENT 1

Materials
Sandpaper
Tape
3 feet (1 m) of string
A 1-liter soda bottle filled with water (with cap tightly
     closed)
A smooth surface such as a linoleum or tile floor

Procedure
1. Tape the sandpaper, gritty side up, to the floor.
2. Tie one end of the string around the middle of the
     soda bottle.
3. Place the soda bottle on
     top of the sandpaper.
4. Try to move the bottle
     off of the sandpaper
     by slowly pulling it
     with the string. Pay
     attention to how much
     force you must exert
     before the bottle
     starts to move and how
     much you must exert to
     keep it moving.

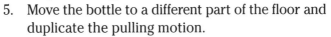

5. Move the bottle to a different part of the floor and
     duplicate the pulling motion.

Results
It should have been more difficult to move the bottle
when it was on the sandpaper. Because the floor is
smoother than the sandpaper, there is less friction
between the floor and the bottle than there is between
the sandpaper and the bottle. One way to reduce friction is by making surfaces smooth.

SANDPAPER

Sandpaper uses friction to smooth down rough pieces of wood or other materials.

Examine some sandpaper in the hardware store. The grit (the cutting material) is very fine on some sandpapers and very coarse on others. The coarse grit removes more material with each stroke, but leaves a rougher surface. The finer the grit, the smoother the finish. Some sandpaper is so fine that it is used to get rid of the fine brushstrokes still visible after an automobile is painted.

Some sandpaper is actually made from a woven cloth, rather than paper, so that it will be more durable. The grit glued to the sandpaper is usually formed from either aluminum oxide or carborundum.

EXPERIMENT 2

Materials
A piece of scrap wood that is smooth on one side
A piece of fine sandpaper
A piece of coarse sandpaper

Procedure
CAUTION: Do this experiment outside so that you do not get wood dust all over the house!

1. Place the piece of wood on a solid flat surface like a concrete step. Make sure it is not a surface, such as a wooden floor, that the sandpaper can scratch.

2. Hold the wood tightly in place with one hand and rub the coarse sandpaper vigorously across the smooth surface. The powder you produce will be a mixture of wood dust and particles of grit from the sandpaper.
3. Examine the sanded surface carefully.
4. Use the fine sandpaper on the wood, and examine the surface again.

Results
After using the coarse sandpaper, you should see lines that it has left in the wood. After you use the fine sandpaper, many of these deeper lines should disappear. The finer grit smoothes out the surface of the wood by removing the high spots.

FILES

Another tool that uses friction to even out surfaces is the file.

When a metal or wood object has a very uneven surface, it may be faster and easier to use a file. Files are made of hard metal and have many rows of "teeth." If the teeth are scraped along a piece of wood or metal, they

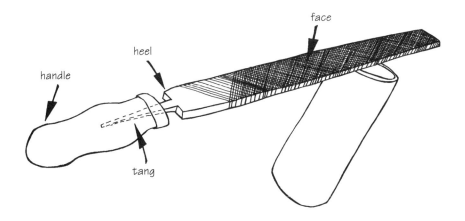

dig into the material and remove small bits of it. Then, as the file is moved back and forth across the surface, more and more of the material is broken up and falls away, leaving a smooth finish.

The more teeth per inch, the smoother the file. Medium-coarse files have about 26 teeth per inch, medium-smooth files have about 38 teeth per inch, and smooth files have about 60 teeth per inch.

LUBRICANTS

When machines operate there is always friction when the surfaces of the various parts come into contact. This friction can cause problems. One way to reduce friction between two surfaces is to coat them with a *lubricant*. Machines such as automobile engines are lubricated with motor oil.

Generally, lubricants coat surfaces that are in contact with each other. The surfaces then ride on a thin layer of the lubricant. Since the lubricant is more slippery than the two surfaces, friction is reduced. Lubricants are also useful because they cool the two surfaces down.

Many of the lubricants sold in hardware stores are liquids such as oils, greases (thicker than oil), and silicone.

Household oil can be very useful. It can lubricate the wheels of a dolly or wheelbarrow, for example. It can also quiet creaking doors and make them easier to open. If friction is causing the door hinges to vibrate and make a spooky creaking noise, put a few drops of household oil on them. This will reduce friction inside the hinges.

Graphite and paraffin wax are popular solid lubricants.

Graphite, the material used to make pencils, is a form of carbon. The structure of these carbon crystals resembles very small, thin plates. Because there is very little friction between these plates, a pencil glides over a piece of paper as you write. But the pencil rubbing against the paper creates enough friction so that some of the graphite is scraped from the pencil and clings to the paper. Graphite is the preferred lubricant for door locks, because unlike the liquid lubricants, it does not attract and hold dust that might clog a lock's delicate mechanism.

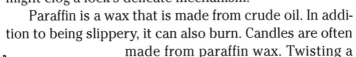

Paraffin is a wax that is made from crude oil. In addition to being slippery, it can also burn. Candles are often made from paraffin wax. Twisting a screw into wood is easier if you rub the screw's threads against a paraffin candle (or a bar of soap) first. Some of the wax will adhere to the threads of the screw. When you twist the screw into the wood, the wax will lubricate the wood and the threads, reducing friction between them and saving you some effort.

Sometimes, water can act as a lubricant.

EXPERIMENT 3

Materials
3 feet (1 m) of string

A 1-liter soda bottle filled with water (with cap tightly closed)

A smooth surface such as a linoleum or tile floor

Procedure

CAUTION: Ask an adult for permission before doing this experiment. Do not do it on a wooden floor because the water may stain the wood.

1. Make a puddle about 8 inches (20 cm) in diameter on a linoleum floor or other smooth surface.
2. Tie one end of the string around the middle of the soda bottle.
3. Place the bottle in the middle of the puddle and pull the string as you did in Experiment 1.

Results

Was it easier to move the bottle when it was standing in the puddle than when it was on a dry floor (recall Experiment 1)? It should have been. The water lubricates the bottom of the bottle, so that it can slide across the floor more easily.

The lubricating action of water is one of the reasons that lifeguards are always telling people to stop running near a swimming pool. Water that is splashed out of the pool makes this area very slippery. If you run on a wet surface like this, you are much more likely to slip, lose your balance, and fall than if you were running on a dry surface.

CHAPTER THREE

Inertia

Every physical substance is made up of *matter*. This includes bowling balls, in-line skates, baseball bats, baseballs, hats, coats, chairs, egg salad sandwiches, soda, ice cream, Twinkies™, soup, and toilet paper.

The only thing in our universe that isn't made up of matter is energy. This includes electricity, rays from the sun, lightning bolts, heat from a fire, and nuclear power.

All matter exhibits *inertia*. In the 1650s, Sir Isaac Newton described inertia in the first of his three laws of

motion. According to this law, "an object in motion will stay in motion in a straight line unless acted upon by an outside force, and an object at rest will stay at rest unless acted upon by an outside force."

The first part of this statement means that if you were in space, way above Earth's atmosphere, and threw a baseball, it would keep going forever, unless it was affected by the gravitational field of a planet, a star, a comet, or a moon.

The second part of Newton's law means that if an object, like a glass of lemonade, were on your kitchen table, it would stay there forever unless something moved it. That something could be you or your mom, or a gust of wind, or even an earthquake.

EXPERIMENT 4

Materials
A ball-peen hammer
Four (4) 1.5-foot (0.5 m) pieces of string (The lengths of string should all be from the same original source so that they will be identical.)

Procedure
CAUTION: Do this experiment outside with adult supervision. Make sure that the hammer does not hit you.
1. Tie one piece of string to a strong, low tree branch. Tie the other end to the head of the hammer with a secure knot.
2. Tie another piece of string to the head of the hammer with a secure knot. The other end of this string should be hanging freely.
3. Slowly pull the loose string straight down until one of the strings breaks. Which one broke—the upper or lower string?

4. Set up the experiment again with the unused pieces of string.
5. Jerk the end of the loose string forcefully downward. Do this until one of the strings breaks. Was it the upper or the lower string?

Results

When you pulled the loose string slowly and steadily, the upper string should have broken first because it has both the force of your hand and the force of *gravity* pulling on it. The lower string is being pulled by the force of your hand only.

When the loose string is pulled with a sudden jerk, the lower string should break first. Because the force you apply is not steady, the lower string must endure the added strain of the hammer's inertia (an object at rest tends to stay at rest). The upper string is not subjected to this extra strain.

OBSERVATION 2

Examine an old hammer. You may notice that the head of the hammer wobbles back and forth a little bit. Here's a trick for tightening the handle temporarily.

Hold the handle of a hammer about halfway between the head and the far end of the handle. Sharply pound the end of the handle against a sturdy solid floor.

Why does this trick work? It has something to do with the inertia of the head of the hammer.

The handle stops abruptly when it comes into contact with the floor. But, since the handle is not mechanically attached to the head of the hammer, the head keeps on moving downward in a straight line until an outside force—the increasing width of the handle—jams it tightly onto the handle and stops its downward motion.

CHAPTER FOUR

The Inclined Plane

As you learned in the Introduction, a plank is one type of inclined plane. Most inclined planes are flat, level, smooth surfaces that are set at an angle. Examples of inclined planes found in a hardware store are axes, hatchets, mauls, nails, chisels, and ladders.

NAILS

A nail's point is an inclined plane, or rather a number of inclined planes. Notice that a nail point usually has four or more sides. Each side is an inclined plane, and they meet at the point.

When you hit the head of a nail with a hammer, all of the force is concentrated on the sharp point. As a result, the point can penetrate a piece of wood. As the nail point moves into the wood, the inclined planes directly behind the point separate or break the wood fibers.

The *elasticity* of the wood allows it to push

tightly against the nail. The friction created between the shaft of the nail and the wood fibers is the force that keeps the nailed pieces together.

EXPERIMENT 5

Materials
Two ten-penny nails
A hammer
A short piece (1 to 2 feet [0.3 to 0.6 m]) of scrap 2 × 4
    lumber
A metal file (used for filing metal)
A ruler

Procedure
CAUTION: Do not perform this experiment without an adult present. Be careful not to smash your fingers.

1. File down the point of one nail until it is completely flat (blunt).
2. Place the 2 × 4 on the floor.
3. With four light blows of the hammer, try to drive the nail that you have filed into the wood. Try to

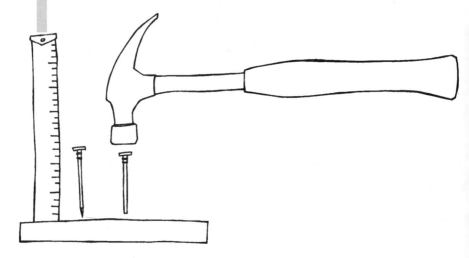

use the same amount of force with each hammer strike. One way to approximate hammer strikes of equal force is to hold the hammer the same distance (measure with the ruler) above each nail head. Rather than smashing the hammer against the nail head, just guide the hammer to it. Let gravity do the work.

4. Now try to drive a nail that still has its point into the same piece of wood.

Results

You should find that the second nail was driven farther into the wood. This experiment demonstrates the usefulness of a nail's inclined planes.

The inclined planes take advantage of the fact that pressure is multiplied as the surface area decreases. If you concentrate all of your force on a very small area (such as a sharp point), you will accomplish more work than if you concentrate all of your force over a large area (such as a point that has been flattened with a file).

AXES, HATCHETS, AND MAULS

CAUTION: These tools can be dangerous. Examine them with extreme care, and do not use them unless an adult is present.
Axes, hatchets, and mauls are usually used to cut, chop, or split wood. Each has a massive, heavy head (made of iron or steel), and a wooden handle. Each head has two or more inclined planes that form a sharp cutting edge. The combination of two inclined planes is sometimes referred to as a wedge. The other side of the head may have a hammer head, another blade, or a flat surface.

The main difference between an axe and a hatchet is the size. The hatchet is a small version of an axe, usually

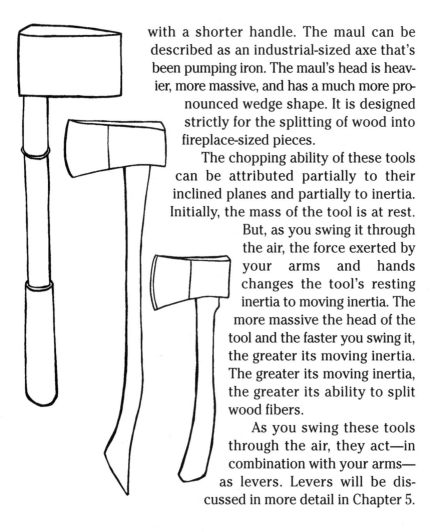

with a shorter handle. The maul can be described as an industrial-sized axe that's been pumping iron. The maul's head is heavier, more massive, and has a much more pronounced wedge shape. It is designed strictly for the splitting of wood into fireplace-sized pieces.

The chopping ability of these tools can be attributed partially to their inclined planes and partially to inertia. Initially, the mass of the tool is at rest. But, as you swing it through the air, the force exerted by your arms and hands changes the tool's resting inertia to moving inertia. The more massive the head of the tool and the faster you swing it, the greater its moving inertia. The greater its moving inertia, the greater its ability to split wood fibers.

As you swing these tools through the air, they act—in combination with your arms— as levers. Levers will be discussed in more detail in Chapter 5.

THE SPLITTING WEDGE

The splitting wedge is similar to the maul, except that it has no handle. It is designed to be hit with a sledge hammer. The blade of a splitting wedge is inserted into a crack in the end of a log or tapped in with a light hammer blow. Once the wedge is in place, it is hit sharply with a sledge hammer. The inclined planes on either side of the blade force the log to split apart.

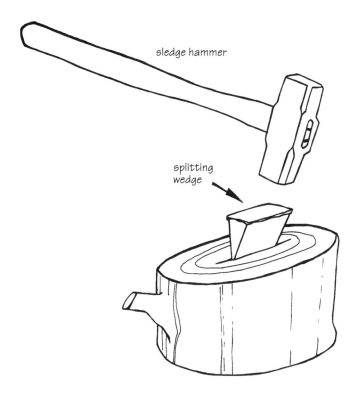

sledge hammer

splitting
wedge

THE COLD CHISEL

The cold chisel is used to cut or break materials other than wood—concrete, metal, hard-packed ground. It is not a precision tool, and is generally used for rough work. Most cold chisels are made from lengths of soft iron bar stock and come to a dull point consisting of two or more inclined planes.

It is called a cold chisel because it is not *tempered* (hardened by application of heat and subsequent quenching in water or oil). The point is placed against the work surface and the other end is hit with a heavy hammer. Due to the shape of the chisel, the force of the hammer blow is applied over a small area. As a result, each blow can break up small areas of hard material.

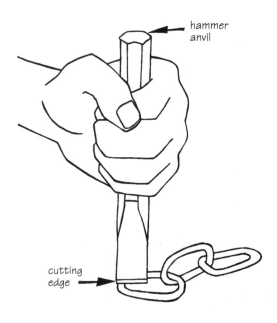

hammer anvil

cutting edge

A cold chisel is often used when a concrete sidewalk or brick wall needs to be repaired. Enlarging the crack allows workers to use enough patching material to fix the fracture properly.

THE WOOD CHISEL

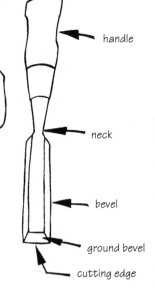

handle

neck

bevel

ground bevel

cutting edge

Unlike the cold chisel, the wood chisel is a precision tool. It is usually made of tempered steel. A wood chisel has a sharp cutting edge at one end and a wood or plastic handle at the other.

You can apply a force to the handle end of a wood chisel by tapping it gently with a hammer or by pressing on it with your hand. The sharp blade gouges or cuts out wood. Experienced craftspeople sometimes use wood chisels to carve intricate patterns into furniture.

THE PLANE

Carpenters use a plane to smooth wood. It is basically a sharp wood chisel that has been placed in a frame. The blade of the chisel sticks out from the bottom of the frame

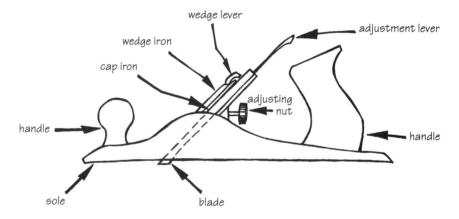

a tiny bit. When the plane is pushed along a piece of wood, the blade shaves off a layer of wood. You can determine exactly how much wood is to be removed by adjusting the blade.

THE WOODEN WEDGE

Have you ever wondered how the head of a hatchet or axe is attached to the handle so that it doesn't fly off when the tool is swung? First, a small slot, about 2 to 3 inches (5 to 8 cm) in length, is cut down the central axis of the handle. The handle is then pushed through a hole—called the "eye"—in the head of the tool. The end of the handle

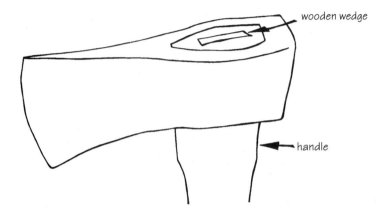

wooden wedge

handle

will stick out from the other side of the head just a little bit.

A wooden wedge is then forced into the slot at the top of the handle. This forces the handle against the inner edges of the eye. The portion of the handle and wedge above the head are cut flush with the head of the tool, and the frictional force holds the handle and head in place.

THE LADDER

How is a ladder an inclined plane? It does not appear to be a flat, level, smooth surface.

Take a look at the illustration (left). A ladder leans against a wall at an angle. For every 1 foot (30 cm) you move vertically (up and down) on the ladder, you also move a certain horizontal (forward and backward) distance. An inclined plane does not always have to be a smooth, flat surface. (A staircase is also an inclined plane.)

CHALLENGE 1

Imagine that you have to deliver two packages that weigh 20 pounds (9 kg) each to two identical buildings. To deliver the packages, you must enter the front doorway of each building. Each door is set into a plain wall and is 5.0 feet (1.5 m) above the ground. Building 1 has a set of steps leading up to the doorway. Building 2 has no steps, just the doorway in the wall. Would you rather deliver the package to Building 1 or Building 2?

Most people would rather deliver the package to the building with the steps. All you would have to do is walk up the steps and carry your package through the front door.

There are a few different ways to deliver the package to Building 2:

- You could hold the package in your arms, stand at the bottom of the wall, and try to jump up 5.0 feet (1.5 m).
- You could lift the package until it is level with the doorway, and slide it in. Then you would have to climb up yourself to get in the doorway.
- You could hold the package, take a running start, and try to jump high enough to get through the doorway.

The point is that stairs make the job easier because they provide a mechanical advantage.

SCREWS AND BOLTS

Screws and *bolts* hold things together. A screw has a slot or other receptacle in its head that accepts a screwdriver's tip. A bolt is tightened with the aid of a wrench.

Screws and bolts have a special type of inclined plane. Look at the way a screw's threads wrap around its shaft. This shape, called a *helix* (something shaped like a spiral), resembles a stretched out Slinky™.

Nearly all screws and bolts are right handed. This means that to screw them in, you must turn them in a clockwise direction, and to unscrew them, you must turn them in a counter-clockwise direction. Even the general purpose incandescent light bulbs that you use at home have right-handed screw bases. (The New York City subway system uses bulbs with specially designed, left-handed screws, so that people will not steal the bulbs to use at home.)

Because most screws are right-handed, auto mechanics, carpenters, and people all over the world doing their own fix-it projects know how to tighten or loosen screws

OBSERVATION 3

Cut a sheet of notebook paper diagonally in half. What you have are two pieces of paper with edges that look like an inclined plane or wedge. Wrap one piece of paper around a pencil, as shown in the drawing at right. You will see that the inclined plane takes on the shape of a screw.

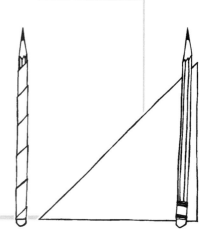

without having to figure out which way to turn the screwdriver.

When I was a youngster, my grandfather taught me a little saying so that I would always know which way to turn a screw: "Lefty loosey, righty tighty." Even though this might sound really dopey, it always helps me to remember which way to turn a screw or bolt.

There are many different types of heads on screws. They may be flat or domed or countersunk. They may be square or round or faceted. There is a type of screwdriver to fit every type of screw. Square and faceted screws can usually be tightened with a wrench.

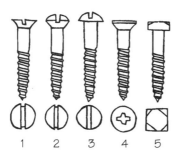

1. flathead
2. oval head
3. roundhead
4. Phillips head
5. lag

The most common kind of screw has a straight slot across the diameter of its head. One problem with the slotted-head screw is that the screwdriver can easily slip out of the slot and strip, or ruin, it. If this happens the screw can not be screwed in or out easily, if at all.

One solution to this problem is the Phillips screwdriver. The Phillips screw slot looks like a four-pointed star. When working in dimly lit places, it is easier to insert the Phillips screwdriver into the star-shaped slot than it is to fit the head of a slotted screwdriver into a slotted screw. In addition, the tip of the Phillips screwdriver tends to stay in place as the screw is tightened because the larger contact area means that there is a greater amount of friction between the screwdriver and the screw's star-shaped receptacle.

The torx head screw offers a positive connection between the screwdriver and the head of the screw. It's frequently found on the fasteners that hold electronic equipment together.

THE WOOD SCREW

A wood screw has a sharp point. If you hold a wood screw against a piece of wood, insert a screwdriver into the slot on top, and twist the handle of the screwdriver in a clockwise direction, the sharp point will start to penetrate the wood. This is why wood screws are said to be self-starting.

As it pierces the wood, the sharp point separates the wood fibers and allows the shaft of the screw to enter the wood. The threads of the screw then grip the wood fibers and pull the screw down into the wood.

Even though wood screws may be self-starting, a small pilot hole is usually drilled into the wood to make it easier for the screw to enter. This also prevents the screw from exerting so much internal pressure that it splits the wood.

MACHINE SCREWS AND NUTS

The machine screw does not have a pointed end. Instead of being screwed into something, it is usually inserted into a predrilled hole, and a nut is then twisted onto it from the opposite side of the drilled material. The threads of the machine screw line up and mesh with the threads on the inside of the nut.

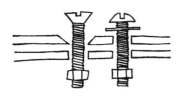

A machine screw/nut combination may be used to fasten objects made of wood, metal, plastic, or concrete. A screwdriver is usually used to twist a machine screw head, and a wrench is used to keep a nut from moving. As the screw and nut are tightened, a considerable amount of force is placed on the material between them. Sometimes this pressure is enough to keep the materials from separating. At other times, the screw and nut are tightened with such force that the threads actually begin to stretch. When this happens, the friction between the screw and the nut may prevent them from coming apart.

If too much pressure is put on a nut and bolt as they are twisted together, however, the bolt may break. Shop manuals for intricate machines such as cars and motorcycles tell you the amount of pressure or *torque* (rotating force) that can safely be applied to each bolt. When an exact amount of force is called for, a torque wrench is used to tighten the bolt. The torque wrench is equipped with a gauge to indicate the force being applied.

Sometimes a *washer* may be inserted between the surface of a material and the screw or bolt head to distribute the pressure over a larger area. This reduces the chance that the screw or bolt head will be pulled through the material.

A lock washer has a special function. By exerting extra pressure on the underside of a screw or bolt head, the washer prevents vibrations from accidentally loosening the screw.

ANCHORS

toggle
(split-wing)

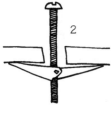

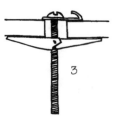

A plastic or lead anchor can help fasten an object to plaster or concrete. The anchor is inserted directly into a hole that has been drilled into the material, and when a screw or bolt is screwed in, the anchor expands and fills the hole.

If you need to attach something to a thin plasterboard wall, you might want to use either a hollow wall anchor (the most well-known brand being the Molly™) or a toggle bolt. You push both of them into the plasterboard through a small drilled hole. The Molly™ "mushrooms" open as the screw is tightened, while the toggle bolt springs open once it is inside the wall. The inner surface of the wall holds the screw or bolt tightly in place.

Molly™
(collapsible anchor)

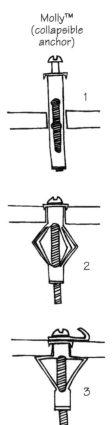

CHAPTER FIVE

The Lever

CHALLENGE 2

Galileo Galilei (1564–1642), a noted Italian scientist, once said that if he could find a place to rest a long enough lever, he could move the Earth. What Galileo really meant was that the scientific principle behind a lever could be applied to an object as massive as the Earth.

Could Earth ever be displaced by a lever? Think of all the problems that you would have to overcome:

- finding a lever that is long enough and strong enough
- finding a fulcrum
- exerting pressure on the lever

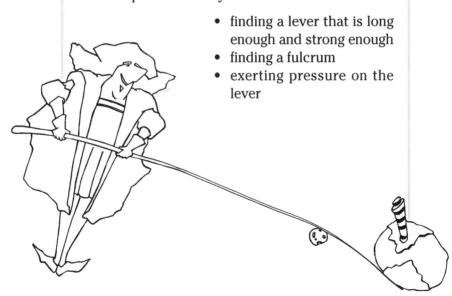

Even if you could find a lever long enough, the person applying force would have to be in outer space. How would that person breathe? Can you come up with some other reasons why it would be difficult, if not impossible, to move the Earth with a lever?

A *lever* is a bar that turns about a pivot point and is used to transfer and/or multiply force. The lever's pivot point is called a *fulcrum*. Levers can help you to multiply input force when you want to accomplish *work*. They can also be used to change the direction of a force or to increase the distance over which an object is moved.

Like inclined planes, levers offer a mechanical advantage. This means that for the input force to be magnified, the object must be moved over a greater distance.

There are three types of levers: first class, second class, and third class. In this chapter, you will learn how each one works and look at some examples.

In a *first-class lever*, such as a teeter-totter or seesaw, the fulcrum is located between the input force and the output force. A first-class lever may have arms of equal or unequal length. If both arms are the same length, the lever can change the direction of the input force. If one arm is longer than the other, the input force can also be magnified.

When the input force is exerted on the longer arm, that arm is pushed down and the shorter or output arm (the resistance) rises. The vertical distance traveled by

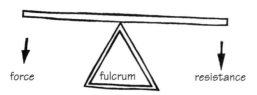

force   fulcrum   resistance

the end of the long arm is greater than the vertical distance traveled by the end of the short arm. As a result, the output force at the end of the short arm is greater than the input force at the end of the long arm.

EXPERIMENT 6

Materials
A 24-inch (66-cm) piece of 2 × 4 lumber
A 6-inch (15-cm) piece of 2 × 4 lumber
A table
A ruler
A 5-pound (2.3-kg) weight (A bag of rice, flour, or nails will work.)
A fisherman's scale
A piece of heavy string

Procedure A
1   Place the short 2 × 4 on the table, as shown in the illustration below. This piece of wood will act as a fulcrum.
2.   Lay the longer 2 × 4 across the fulcrum so that it is balanced (About 11 inches [28 cm] of wood should be hanging over each side of the fulcrum.) Each end of the longer piece of wood will act as one arm of the lever.
3.   Measure and record the vertical distance between each arm of the lever and the tabletop. Use the same point of measurement on each side, either the bottom edge or top edge of the wood.

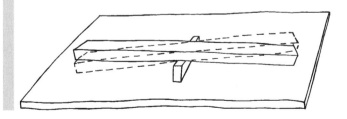

4. While holding the middle of the lever in place, push one arm of the lever down until it touches the tabletop.
5. Measure and record the vertical distance between the raised arm of the lever and the tabletop.
6. Now push the opposite end of the lever down until it touches the tabletop. Measure and record the vertical distance between the raised arm of the lever and the tabletop.

Procedure B
CAUTION: Watch the lever and weight carefully so that they do not fall and injure you.

1. Move the entire lever so that its fulcrum is near the edge of the table and one end of the lever extends beyond the table. (The fulcrum should still be directly under the center of the longer 2 × 4, so that one-half of the longer 2 × 4 extends over the edge of the table top.)
2. Weigh the 5-pound (2.3-kg) weight with the fisherman's scale. It is not important that the scale says exactly 5 pounds (2.3 kg), but it is important to know the exact weight so that your results will be meaningful.
3. Place the weight on the end of the lever that is over the table. That end will now rest on the tabletop.
4. Attach the fisherman's scale to the opposite end of the lever with a loop of string.
5. Pull down on the scale until both arms of the lever are level.
6. Record the measurement shown on the scale. This measurement tells you how much input force was necessary to lift the 5-pound (2.3-kg) weight.

Procedure C

1. Move the fulcrum so that it is closer to the center of the table.
2. Move the arms of the lever until one arm is 7 inches (18 cm) long and the other arm is 15 inches (38 cm) long.
3. Push the short arm of the lever down until it touches the tabletop. Measure and record the vertical distance between the raised arm of the lever and the tabletop.

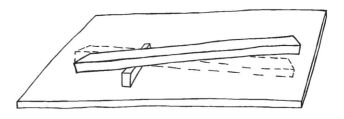

4. Push the long arm of the lever to the tabletop. Measure and record the vertical distance between the raised arm of the lever and the tabletop.

Procedure D

1. Move the entire fulcrum so that the long arm of the lever extends 2 inches (5 cm) over the table's edge.
2. Place the weight on the short end of the lever.
3. Attach the fisherman's scale to the long arm of the lever with a loop of string.

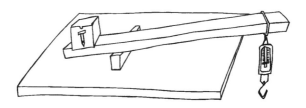

4. Pull down on the scale until the two ends of the lever are level. Record the weight shown on the scale.
5. Reverse the lever so that the longer arm is resting on the table and the shorter arm extends 2 inches (5 cm) over the table's edge.

6. Place the weight at the end of the long arm.
7. Attach the fisherman's scale to the short arm of the lever with a loop of string.
8. Pull down on the scale until the two ends of the lever are level. Measure and record how much force is needed to make the lever level.

Results

Look over all of the data you have recorded. When the lever was balanced on the fulcrum and both arms were the same length, the vertical distance between the tabletop and each raised arm was equal. The force needed to make the lever arms level was equal to the weight of the object.

When the arms of the lever were unequal and the arm was pushed down, the vertical distance between the tabletop and the short arm was half the vertical distance between the long arm and the tabletop when the short arm was pushed down. When the weight was on the short arm, the force required to move it was equal to one-half its weight. When the weight was on the long arm, the force required to move it was about twice its weight.

This experiment was designed to demonstrate the

usefulness of the first-class lever in magnifying force and distance. The mechanical advantage offered by the longer arm of the lever is about 2 to 1. The force required to move the 5-pound (2.3-kg) weight is about 2.5 pounds (1.2 kg).

The hardware store has many examples of first-class levers.

THE CLAW HAMMER (AS A NAIL PULLER)

Before looking at the illustration, try to figure out how a hammer can act as a first-class lever? When the claw-end is hooked under a nail's head and the handle is forced down in an arc, the force at the handle's end is multiplied, making it easy to extract the nail. The distance traveled by the long arm, the handle, is much greater than the distance traveled by the short arm, the claw. The center of the hammer's head, the part that the handle passes through, becomes the fulcrum.

THE PRY BAR

When the short end of a pry bar is placed under an object and a block of wood or a brick is used to support the fulcrum, the input force can be multiplied many times. This is why it is possible to move extremely heavy objects with a pry bar.

Imagine that a farmer wants to move a heavy rock in her field. Using a pry bar would make the job much easier. The farmer would shove one end of a pry bar as far under the rock as possible, then place a piece of wood or a brick (the fulcrum) between the end of the bar that is wedged

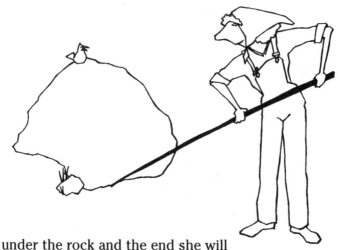

under the rock and the end she will
push down. When the farmer applies a force
to the pry bar, it will be multiplied, allowing her to move
the rock. The closer the fulcrum is to the end of the pry
bar that is underneath the rock, the more her input force
will be magnified.

PLIERS, TIN SNIPS, AND SCISSORS

Pliers, tin snips, and scissors all work the same way. They
consist of two first-class levers connected at their pivot
points. You can see this for yourself by doing the following
experiment.

EXPERIMENT 7

Materials
A pair of pliers
A tabletop

Procedure
1. Rest one handle of a pair of pliers on the edge of a
    table so that the gripping part hangs over the
    edge.

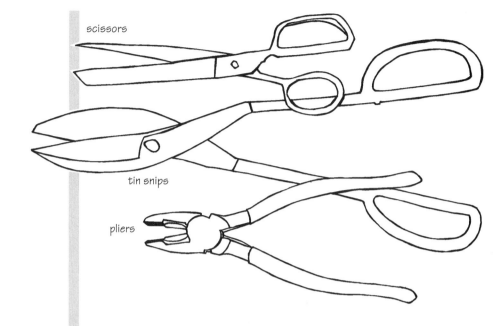

scissors

tin snips

pliers

2. With the fingers of your right hand, hold the handle firmly against the tabletop.
3. With your left hand, move the other handle up and down.
4. Repeat steps 1–3 using the other handle.

Results
Because the input arms (handles) are much longer than the output arms (jaws), the force exerted on the handles is magnified at the jaws. Notice how much farther the end of the handles move than the end of the jaw. Think back to the experiments that you conducted with first-class levers. Those results will help you understand why this type of tool magnifies input force. Since you could perform the experiment while pressing either handle against the tabletop, you know that a pair of pliers is a combination of two first-class levers.

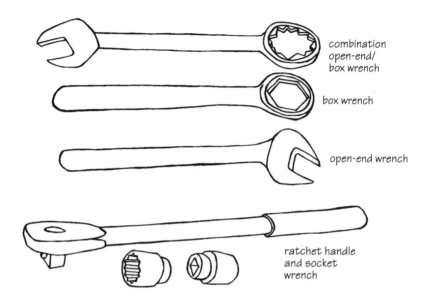

combination
open-end/
box wrench

box wrench

open-end wrench

ratchet handle
and socket
wrench

WRENCHES

A wrench is basically a first-class lever with a round or U-shaped receptacle that fits tightly around a nut or bolt in order to tighten it. The wrench's long span is the input-force arm. The output force is concentrated at the receptacle, which grasps the nut or bolt. The fulcrum is at the center of the nut or bolt, so it falls between the input and output arms.

There are three types of simple wrenches—open-ended wrenches, box wrenches, and socket wrenches. An open-ended wrench is not quite as strong as a box wrench, but it is more versatile because it can fit into places that a box wrench can't. The box wrench must be placed over a nut or bolt, while the open-ended wrench can be placed alongside a nut or bolt.

Socket wrenches are quite useful, at times almost indispensable. The head of a socket wrench fits over the top of a bolt or nut, so a deep socket wrench may be able to tighten bolts in long or narrow holes where open-ended

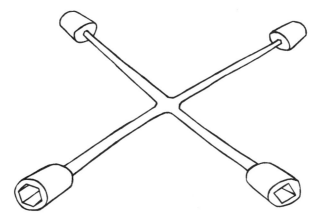

and box wrenches can't reach. One type of socket wrench, for example, is designed to tighten spark plugs inside automobile or motorcycle engines.

The lug wrench is a type of socket wrench. It is used to tighten and loosen automobile lug nuts, which keep the wheels of an automobile attached to their axle, so that they don't fall off the car. A lug wrench is usually built in the shape of a cross, with a different-shaped socket on each end of the cross.

This shape allows a mechanic to apply an input force with both arms, so that when the lug nuts are replaced, enough force will be applied to keep any vibrations from loosening them.

In a *second-class lever*, the fulcrum is at one end, while the input force is applied at the other end and the opposing force is at the center.

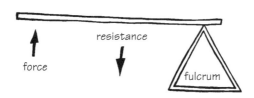

EXPERIMENT 8

Materials

A 24-inch (66-cm) piece of 2 × 4 lumber
A table
A yardstick or meter stick
A 5-pound (2.3-kg) weight (A bag of rice, flour, or nails
   will work.)
A fisherman's scale
A piece of heavy string

Procedure

1. Weigh the 5-pound (2.3-kg) weight to establish the
   scale's accuracy.
2. Place the 2 × 4 on the tabletop, wide side down.
3. Tie the string around one end of the 2 × 4. (The
   other end acts as the fulcrum.)
4. Place the weight 8 inches (20 cm) from the fulcrum.

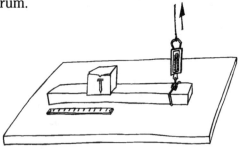

5. Attach the scale to the string loop and use it to
   lift the end of the input arm approximately 6
   inches (15 cm) off the tabletop. Record the weight.
6. Place the weight 12 inches (30 cm) from the fulcrum and use the scale to lift the end of the input
   arm off the tabletop. Record the weight.
7. Place the weight 16 inches (40 cm) from the fulcrum and use the scale to lift the end of the input
   arm off the tabletop. Record the weight.
8. Place the weight 24 inches (60 cm) from the ful-

crum (at the very end of the input arm) and use the scale to lift the end of input arm off the table-top. Record the weight.

Results

Compare the forces needed to lift the weight at different distances from the fulcrum. This will give you an indication of the mechanical advantage that a second-class lever offers. If you have a longer 2 × 4, try the experiment again. (You should first measure the force needed to lift one end of the longer 2 × 4 with no weight on the board.)

SPRING CLAMPS

Look at the illustration below and try to figure out how a spring clamp functions as both a first- and a second-class lever. As you squeeze the handles to clamp something together, the spring exerts a force between the end of the

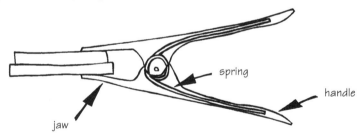

handles and the pivot point. In other words, the clamp acts as a second-class lever. As soon as you let go of the handle, however, the spring clamp becomes a first-class lever. The force of the spring is on one side of the fulcrum and the resistance is between the jaws of the clamp.

THE WHEELBARROW

It is quite obvious why a wheelbarrow is a second-class lever. You exert an input force on the handles, the load

(opposing force) is in the barrow, and the wheel and axle act as a fulcrum.

THE PRY BAR

The pry bar can also be used as either a first- or second-class lever. Suppose that a farmer wants to move a giant boulder. She could slip one end of the pry bar under the boulder and instead of placing a brick or piece of wood under the pry bar, pull up on it. In this case, the ground acts as the fulcrum. The opposing force (the rock) is between the fulcrum and the end to which the input force is applied.

The *third-class lever* has the fulcrum at one end, the opposing force at the other end, and the input force in the mid-

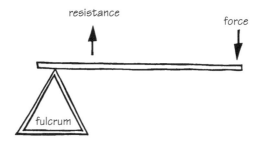

dle. Some of the tools you have already learned about can be used as third-class levers.

THE HAMMER (AS A NAIL DRIVER)

When you use a hammer to drive nails, split wood with a splitting wedge, or carve wood with a chisel, the hammer acts as a third-class lever in combination with your arm. The hand holding the handle of the hammer is the source of input force, your wrist acts as the fulcrum, and the object being hit is the opposing force. (Make sure the object you hit is not your thumb!!)

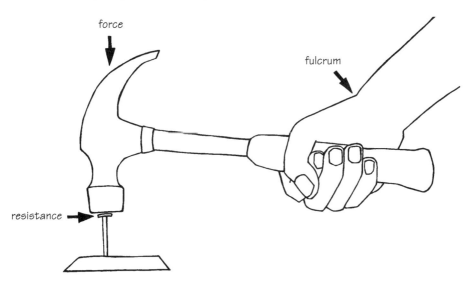

THE PRY BAR

The pry bar can also be a third-class lever. Firemen frequently use pry bars in this way. If a fireman has to knock down overhanging timber, he might hold onto the pry bar at one end and swing it like a baseball bat at the piece of wood. In this case, his hand exerts the input force, his wrist acts as the fulcrum, and the timber acts as the opposing force.

CHAPTER SIX

The Wheel and Axle

The wheel may be thought of as a donut-shaped object with a center. The center is solid and attached to a rod or bar called the axle, and together the wheel and axle act as a single tool. This tool reduces friction. It also allows input force and input speeds to be magnified.

How does the wheel magnify input speed? As a wheel rotates, the outer portion of the wheel (the *circumference*) moves a greater distance than the inner portion of the wheel. This greater movement provides a mechanical advantage.

Have you ever noticed that the steering wheel of a school bus is much larger than the steering wheel of a car? If you've ever gone to a museum that has antique cars, you might have noticed that the steering wheels in those cars are also larger than the steering wheels in cars made today. Before power steering was invented, steering an automobile was much more difficult, and it required more muscle than steering today's cars. A larger steering wheel made the cars easier to maneuver. Of course larger steering wheels also meant that the drivers had to move their hands in larger circles.

EXPERIMENT 9

Materials
A brass outdoor faucet with a circular handle
A screwdriver

Procedure
1. Remove the screw from the center of the handle and take the handle off the faucet. (Do not lose the screw.)
2. Using your finger, try to turn the axle (the part of the faucet that connects the handle to the faucet).
3. Now, replace the handle (including the screw) and twist it.

Results
You should have noticed that it is much easier to open and close the faucet with the handle in place. This is because the faucet handle magnifies the input force. (Maintenance people often remove the handle of an outside faucet to prevent unauthorized water use.)

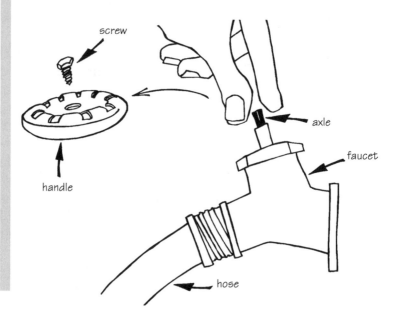

The wheel can be considered a circular lever. A line running through the diameter of the wheel can be considered the arm of the lever.

Some people think that the wheel was the most important invention ever—more important than popcorn, MTV, the surfboard, or even ice cream. It's such a simple idea that it is hard to believe it hasn't existed forever. One reason it had to be invented is that it generally doesn't exist in nature.

None of the animals we can see with the naked eye, for example, use wheels to move from one place to another. Dogs, cats, and horses have legs, birds have wings, and fish have fins. Maybe someone came up the idea for the wheel when they saw a tree trunk start to roll down a hill.

But just think of all the things that would not exist if the wheel hadn't been invented. There would be no cars, no buses, no subways, no trains, no bicycles, no motorcycles, no in-line skates, no electric motors, no go-carts, and no Big-Wheels™ for little kids to ride. This is just the beginning of the list.

Many of the items you'll find in a hardware store have wheels. Wheel barrows, moving dollies, casters, and adjustable wrenches are just a few examples.

CASTERS

A caster is a small wheel that is permanently attached to the bottom of a cart or a piece of furniture. In addition to a wheel, you will also find a bearing attached to the caster, which allows the caster to swivel. There are many different designs for casters, but they all do the same thing. They all reduce friction so that heavy items can be moved easily.

Many chairs, especially desk chairs, have casters. The casters on the bottom of a desk chair allow you to move across a room without getting up. The casters on the legs

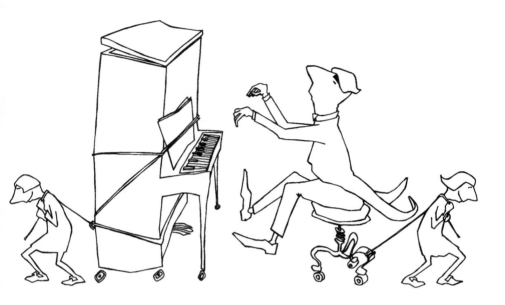

of a piano allow stagehands to move it from one part of a concert hall to another. The casters on the bottom of a cart allow warehouse workers to move large boxes or heavy machinery with relative ease.

THE WHEELBARROW

As you learned in Chapter 5, a wheelbarrow acts as a second-class lever in which the wheel is the fulcrum. The wheel of the wheelbarrow reduces friction, which makes it even easier for you to move a heavy load.

THE SCREWDRIVER

Before you read any further, try to figure out which part of a screwdriver acts as a wheel. Give up? The handle of the screwdriver is actually a wheel. As you turn the handle, it spins around and around just like a wheel, magnifying the input force that you apply to it with the twisting motion of your wrist. The shaft of the screwdriver functions as the axle.

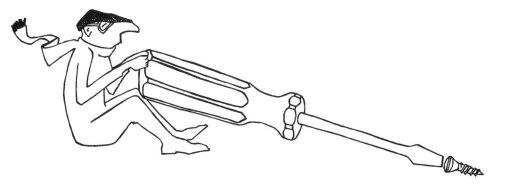

EXPERIMENT 10

Materials

A screw
A screwdriver
A piece of paper
A ruler
A marking pen

Procedure

1. With a marking pen, draw an arrow on the head of the screw pointing to the edge of the head.
2. Place the screw on the piece of paper so that the arrowhead is touching the paper.
3. Mark the screw's position on the piece of paper.
4. Roll the screw in a straight line until the head has made one full revolution. Mark that point on the paper, too.
5. Now, using the marking pen, make a dot on the top edge of the screwdriver handle.
6. Place the screwdriver on the piece of paper so that the dot is touching the paper. Mark the position of the dot on the paper.
7. Roll the handle of the screwdriver across the paper until it has made one full revolution and mark the final position of the dot.
8. Measure the length of one full revolution of the

screw and one full revolution of the screwdriver handle.

Results

You will see that the distance the screwdriver handle travels during one revolution is much greater than the distance the screw head travels in one revolution. If you divide the distance the handle traveled by the distance the screw head traveled, the result will be the mechanical advantage provided by the screwdriver.

EXPERIMENT 11

Materials

A block of wood
A drill with a 1/16-inch bit
A wood screw
A screwdriver

Procedure

1. Drill a 1/16-inch hole in a small block of wood.
2. Insert the tip of a wood screw into the hole.
3. Try to turn the head of the screw with your finger and thumb.
4. Next, place the screwdriver in the slot on top of the screw.
5. Try to turn the screw by turning the shaft of the screwdriver.
6. Now try to twist the screw in while turning the handle of the screwdriver.

Result

You will find it difficult to grasp and twist the head of the screw with your finger and thumb because it is so small, and because the screw is made of a material that is harder than your fingertips. It is also difficult to turn the screw when you grasp the shaft of the screwdriver because it is thin and smooth. There is very little friction to keep your hand from slipping.

Twisting the screw is much easier, though, when you hold on to the handle. Screwdriver handles are made of wood or plastic and usually have grooves. Friction exists between your hand and the handle. As a result, it does not slip out of your hand. You can grasp the handle tightly and exert a great deal of force on it. In addition, the wide diameter of the handle gives you a considerable mechanical advantage.

THE CIRCULAR SAW

CAUTION: Saws are extremely dangerous. Use them only when an adult is present. If you are not very careful, you may injure or even lose a finger or limb.

Saws are used to cut wood, metal, plastics, and other materials. Saws work because they are harder than the substance that they are cutting, and as a result they are able to break the bonds between the molecules of the material being cut.

A hand saw cuts through a piece of wood with a back and forth motion. The faster the saw blade moves back and forth, the more often the teeth of the blade attack or bite into the wood in a given period of time, and the faster the wood gets cut.

The blade of a circular saw is a wheel. Because the blade is a wheel, you do not have to change the direction of movement at the end of each cutting stroke. As a result, the teeth can bite into the wood at a faster rate than the teeth of a hand saw.

The axle of this wheel is at the output shaft of an elec-

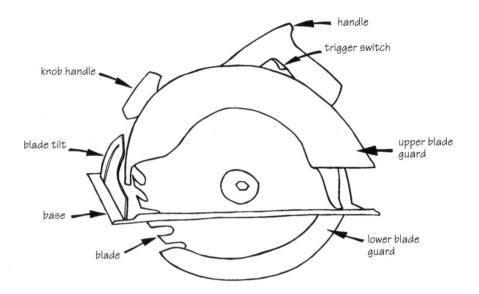

handle

trigger switch

knob handle

blade tilt

base

blade

upper blade guard

lower blade guard

tric motor. The axle of the saw moves at a slower speed than the outer circumference of the blade. Although the axle and teeth of the blade rotate at the same rate (number of revolutions per minute), the teeth of the blade must actually move faster than the axle because the teeth must travel a greater distance than the axle in the same amount of time.

THE BRACE

A brace is a type of drill that is used to bore large-diameter holes through wood. At first glance, a brace may not look like a wheel. That's because most of the wheel's circumference is missing.

When you use a brace, the handle rotates through a large circle (the wheel). But the cutting part of the brace, which is called the bit, moves in a much smaller circle (the axle). As a result, the input force you exert on the handle is magnified.

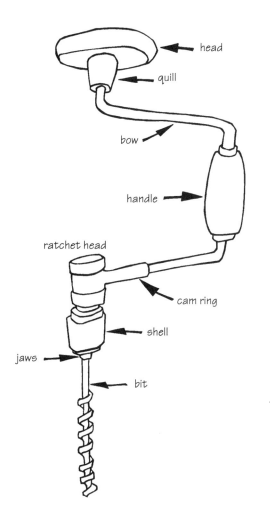

THE HAND DRILL

A hand drill has a special type of wheel called a *gear*. In this case, the gear is a wheel with teeth along its outer edge. These teeth decrease slippage. Gears usually mesh with other gears, but they may sometimes mesh with a chain. This happens in chainsaws and bicycles. Like any wheel, gears can increase the mechanical advantage and change the direction of the input forces.

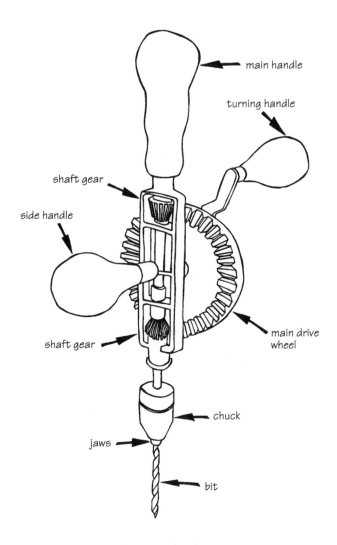

main handle

turning handle

shaft gear

side handle

shaft gear

main drive
wheel

chuck

jaws

bit

When the handle of the hand drill's drive wheel is turned, the toothed surface of the gear comes into contact with the teeth of a smaller gear called the shaft gear. The movement of teeth on the drive wheel causes the shaft gear to move in a circle. The shaft gear is connected to the *chuck* (an adjustable drill bit holder) and drill bit. When you turn the handle of the drill, the drill bit begins to spin, and the sharpened end of the bit enters the object beneath it. *Helixes* above the point of the bit pull the left-over dust away from the hole.

Because the drive wheel of the drill shown on the previous page is much larger than the shaft gear, it has at least three times more teeth. For every complete revolution that the drive wheel makes, the shaft gear revolves at least three times. As a result, the shaft, chuck, and drill bit are all turning three times faster than the handle. Thus, the mechanical advantage of this particular drill is 3:1.

CHAPTER SEVEN

The Pulley

A pulley is another special type of wheel. The axle of the wheel is attached to a cagelike device, called a *bale*, and the outer circumference of the wheel is grooved to hold a rope or cable in place. The wheel itself may be made of wood, metal, or plastic.

SIMPLE PULLEYS

A simple pulley can be used to change the direction of an applied force. For example, you can lift a bucket full of bricks to the top floor of a building by pulling down on a rope that has been threaded through a pulley attached to the roof. It requires much less work to lift the bricks using a pulley than to carry them up several flights of stairs.

Let's imagine that you and your sister are moving the bricks. To use the pulley, you must first find a long rope—one more than twice the height of the building. After threading the rope through the pulley, you can attach a bucket to one end of the rope and tie a knot at the other end.

Now you can load the bricks into the bucket at ground level, then pull on the end of the rope with a knot in it. Your sister, who is at the top of the building, unloads the bricks and lowers the bucket back to you.

By using the pulley to change the direction of the force (you pulled down on the rope and the bricks went up), you saved energy. If you and your sister had carried the bricks up the stairs, you would have had to exert enough energy to lift not just the bricks but yourselves, too.

Window Shades

Sometimes, small pulleys and ropes are used to raise window shades in school classrooms. The shade goes up when you pull down on the cord. These pulleys also help

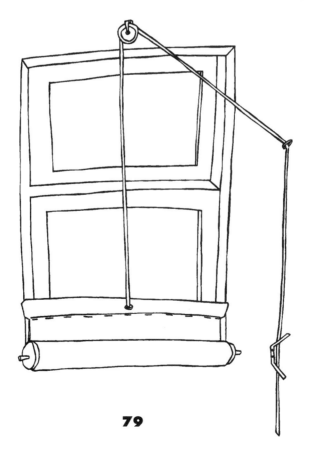

you to save your own energy because if the pulley system was not there, you would have to go find a ladder, bring it back, climb to the top of the window, and then pull the shade up.

COMPOUND PULLEYS

A compound pulley or *block and tackle* can multiply and change the direction of an applied force. The simplest compound pulley has two wheels, one at the top and one at the bottom. The wheels revolve around an axle.

As is the case with an inclined plane and a lever, increasing input force means that the force exerted on

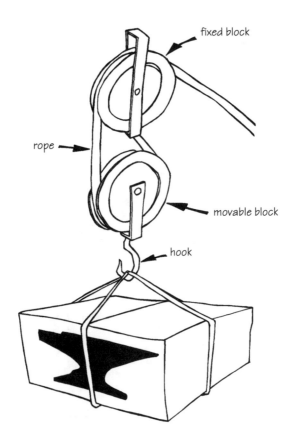

fixed block

rope

movable block

hook

the rope or cable must travel a greater distance. To magnify the input force five times, you must pull the rope five times farther than the object being lifted moves. For every 5 feet (1.5 m) of rope that you pull through the system, the output force increases by 1 foot (30 cm).

EXPERIMENT 12

Materials
Two strong wooden poles about 1 yard (1 m) long
A 30-foot (10-m) piece of strong rope
Two friends

Procedure
1. Tie one end of the rope 12 inches (30 cm) from the end of one pole.
2. While your friends hold the poles parallel to each other and about 3 feet (1 m) apart, loop the rope around the poles seven times.
3. Tell your friends to try as hard as they can to keep the poles from being pulled together as you pull steadily on the free end of the rope.

Results

After pulling on the rope for a few moments, the poles will start to move toward each other. Your friends will be unable to keep the poles apart. This is because the poles and rope act as a block and tackle. Your input strength is being multiplied seven times by this compound pulley.

CHAPTER EIGHT

Combination Tools

ADJUSTABLE WRENCHES

Adjustable wrenches, including the monkey wrench and the Crescent® wrench, are special types of open-ended wrenches. They take advantage of two simple tools: the screw and the lever.

While many wrenches are designed to fit only one size nut or bolt, adjustable wrenches can fit many sizes. Their screw mechanism, known as a worm screw, makes them extremely versatile. The worm screw engages a "rack" on either the jaw or shaft of the wrench. This rack consists of a series of grooves that mesh with the spiral of the worm. As the adjusting worm is turned, the jaw opens and closes. Look at the illustration on the next page to see the locations of the fixed jaw, movable jaw, and worm screw on a monkey wrench and a Crescent wrench®.

Once the jaw has been adjusted, the wrench is used as a first-class lever to tighten or loosen nuts and bolts. The wrench's long handle is the input force arm. The output force is applied at the receptacle (the jaws). The center of the nut or bolt acts as a fulcrum. Since the receptacle surrounds the nut or bolt, the fulcrum falls between the input and output arms.

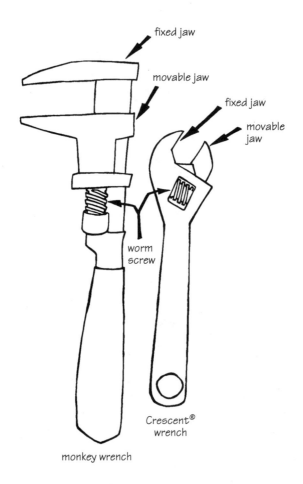

fixed jaw

movable jaw

fixed jaw

movable jaw

worm screw

Crescent® wrench

monkey wrench

VISES

The vise holds an object in place so that your hands are free to cut, drill, or plane it. Like the adjustable wrench, the vise is a lever-and-screw mechanism. The handle is a lever that turns a screw mechanism, pulling the jaws of the vise together. The jaws apply pressure evenly to the object being held. If the object in the vise is delicate, you can protect it by placing a soft cloth over the jaws.

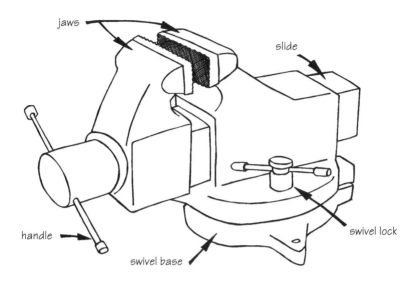

jaws

slide

handle

swivel base

swivel lock

THE VISE GRIP®

A vise grip® is a type of pliers. It uses a combination of levers to increase the force applied to the object being

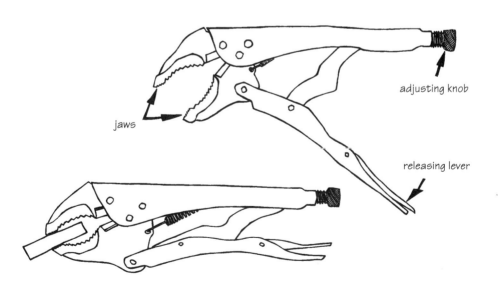

jaws

adjusting knob

releasing lever

gripped. A screw-and-spring mechanism can be used to adjust the distance between the jaws.

One arm of this tool is solid and acts as a simple first-class lever. An adjusting screw at the back of this solid arm opens and closes a set of jaws. The other arm of the tool is a compound lever—a combination of two first-class levers—that increases the input force and allows the pliers to lock onto the object. A third first-class lever is used to release the locking mechanism.

BOLT CUTTERS

Bolt cutters are available in a number of sizes. The larger the bolt cutter, the larger and sturdier the lock that they can cut.

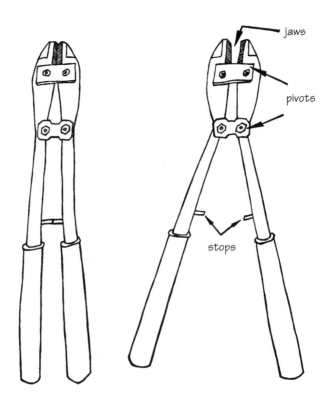

jaws

pivots

stops

A bolt cutter is a combination of levers and inclined planes. Both arms of this tool are compound levers. The input arms are much longer than the cutting edges (output arms), so the result is a large mechanical advantage.

The long levers in the input arms move two additional levers that multiply the input force even more. The combined output force is then concentrated on the cutting edges. The cutting edges, which are inclined planes, are usually made of hardened steel. The combination of the magnified input force and the hardened-steel jaws allows this tool to cut through the average bolt with ease.

CHAPTER NINE

Mass, Weight, and Gravity

Mass is the measure of the amount of matter inside an object. This matter is made up of *atoms* and *molecules*.

In Chapter 3, you learned about Newton's laws of motion. You can think of mass as a measure of the inertial force needed to stop a moving object or to move an object at rest. In other words, the more massive (the more matter inside) an object, the more difficult it is to change that object's state of motion or state of rest.

Gravity is an attractive force that exists between all objects in the universe. In this case, attractive doesn't mean cute, huggable, or adorable, it means pulling toward each other. Gravity is the reason that apples fall to the ground instead of floating up into the sky. Earth attracts the apple and the apple attracts Earth. Gravity is what holds you to the surface of the Earth. If there were no gravity, you would float into space.

Sir Isaac Newton is the scientist who mathematically defined gravity. Before Newton, many people thought that things fell to the ground because that was their proper place—it was where they belonged. Luckily, we now have a better understanding of gravity.

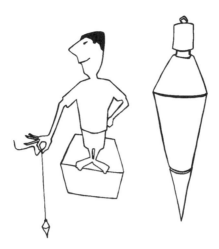

THE PLUMB LINE

One tool that takes advantage of gravity is the plumb line, which is used by masons and carpenters to establish a true vertical. When you hold one end of the string in your hand, the weight at the other end of the plumb line (the plumb bob) is drawn toward the center of the Earth by gravity. As a result, the line created by the string is perfectly vertical.

It might interest you to know that the words plumb and plumbing come from the Latin word for lead. Plumbing pipes and plumb bobs used to be made of lead.

THE FISHERMAN'S SCALE

Weight is the measure of how much force is being exerted between Earth's mass and the mass of the object being pulled down to Earth by gravity. Weight is usually measured with a scale. You might be able to find a fisherman's scale in the hardware store.

This scale consists of a hollow box that is suspended from a hook. Inside the box is a cylinder. At the top of the cylinder is a pointer that can be seen through a slot in the box. Inside the cylinder is a spring. The bottom of the spring is attached to another hook.

The manufacturer calculated how much the spring will stretch for each ounce of weight added to the hook, then put those numbers in the appropriate place—next to the slots where the pointer is visible.

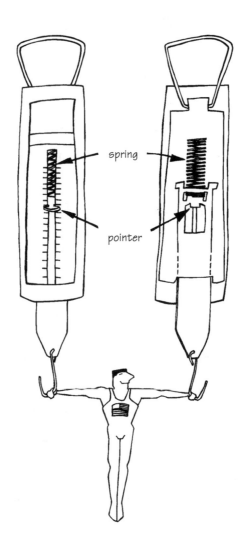

spring

pointer

Buoyancy

If something is *buoyant* it will float in water or in another liquid. If it is not buoyant, it will not float.

THE LEVEL

A level can be used to determine whether a surface is perfectly horizontal or vertical. Most levels consist of a rectangular frame that contains two or more liquid-filled compartments. Within each compartment is an air bubble. The bubble moves to the center of the tube when the level is set on a perfectly flat surface. One compartment indicates whether a surface is perfectly horizontal, and the other indicates whether a surface is perfectly vertical.

A level takes advantage of buoyancy. Because the air bubbles are more buoyant than the liquid in each of the compartments, they float on top. Each compartment has

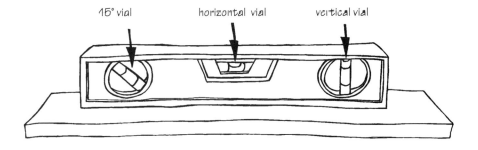

45° vial   horizontal vial   vertical vial

a small curve in it, and the middle of the curve is the highest point in the compartment. When the bubble is at the exact center of the compartment (at the highest point), you know that the surface is perfectly level.

CHAPTER ELEVEN

Cutting Tools

We all know that sharp things cut. But what does that really mean? Think of all the cutting tools that you have learned about in other parts of this book. The bolt cutter, scissors, and tin snips all consist of levers. A hand drill has gears (a type of wheel).

If you think about it, all of these tools could have been discussed in the chapter on combination tools. They consist of levers or wheels as well as a very basic tool, the inclined plane. All cutting tools—including the axe, hatchet, splitting edge, and maul—have inclined planes. These inclined planes make the cutting edge sharp. *Sharpness* is a measure of how fine the edge of a tool is.

Can everything with inclined planes cut? No. If a frozen stick of butter had inclined planes at one end it wouldn't be able to cut a piece of wood or your finger. (It might be able to cut through cottage cheese.) At room temperature, a stick of butter probably couldn't cut anything.

Besides being sharp, a cutting edge must also be harder than the material it is cutting. A material's *hardness* is determined by its ability to scratch other materials. Harder materials can scratch softer ones, but softer materials cannot scratch harder ones.

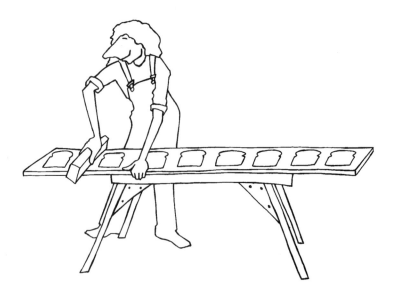

A diamond is the hardest known *mineral*. It can cut anything. Ideally, all cutting surfaces would be made of diamond. Unfortunately, though, diamonds are very rare. As a result, they are very expensive—too expensive to be used to make all cutting surfaces.

Friederich Mohs (1773–1839), a German mineralogist, developed a scale that rates the hardness of ten different minerals: diamond, corundum, topaz, quartz, orthoclase, apatite, fluorite, calcite, gypsum, and talc. Each mineral listed can be scratched by the minerals listed before it. The softest material on the list, talc, is used to make talcum powder.

Most of the cutting edges of tools found in a hardware store are made of steel, including hacksaws, crosscut saws, ripsaws, drill bits, wood chisels, and wood planes. The average steel saw blade used to cut wood measures about 6 on the Mohs' Scale. (Your fingernail measures about 2.)

Many of us have had the painful experience of getting a paper cut. Did you ever wonder how the heck paper can cut our skin? If you look at the edge of a piece of paper, you will see that it is thin. This also makes it fairly sharp, and because paper is harder than your skin, under the right conditions it can slice it, sometimes causing a deep cut.

CHAPTER TWELVE

Pressure

Pressure measures the amount of force applied over a certain area. Air pressure is the force exerted by air on a surface. Water pressure is the force exerted by water on a surface.

Pressure is usually measured in pounds per square inch (lbs./in^2), ounces per square inch (ozs./in^2), grams per square centimeter (g/cm^2), or kilograms per square centimeter (kg/cm^2). If you stood a 2 pound (1 kg) brick on its end, the pressure exerted on the floor by the brick would be 2 pounds (1 kg) divided by the number of square inches occupied by the brick. If you stood the brick on one of its wider sides, the total weight of the brick remains the same, but the pressure is less because that weight is spread out over a larger surface area.

Suppose that the bottom of a 100-ounce box of carpenter's nails is resting on a tabletop. The measurements of the box are 5 inches × 5 inches × 2 inches. How much pressure is the box exerting on the tabletop? Since you know the dimensions of the box, you can determine the surface area of its bottom side (5 inches × 5 inches = 25 square inches). To find out how much pressure the box is exerting on the table, you can divide this surface area by the weight of the box (100 ounces ÷ 25 square inches = 4 ounces/square inch).

If you turn the box of nails on its narrow side, the

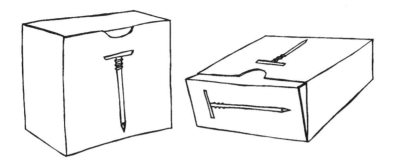

weight of the box remains the same, but the surface area changes (5 inches × 2 inches = 10 square inches). Since the surface area changes, so does the amount of pressure being exerted on the tabletop (100 ounces ÷ 10 square inches = 10 ounces/square inch).

Note how the pressure increases as the surface area decreases, even though the weight remains the same.

THE NAIL AND THE AXE

As you learned in Chapter 4, the wedge found on the point of a nail or the blade of an axe takes advantage of the fact that pressure is multiplied as the surface area decreases. In both cases, the input force (pressure per square inch) is much greater at the tip of the wedge than it would be on a flatter surface.

AUTOMOBILE JACKS

Some automobile jacks have a closed *hydraulic* system. This system takes advantage of the properties of pressure to lift cars off the ground so that you can change a flat tire.

Look at the illustration below. For the sake of this explanation, let's say that Container A has a surface area of 1 and Container B has a surface area of 10. Each con-

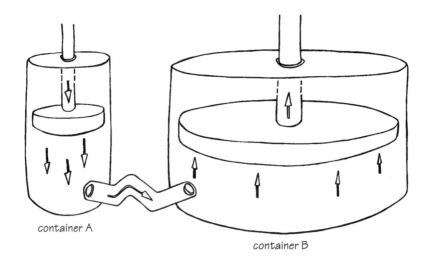

container A

container B

tainer is filled with oil and connected through a tube. Containers A and B both have oil-tight pistons that prevent the oil from leaking.

As the piston in Container A is pushed down, the oil inside the container is forced through the tube into Container B. As a result, the piston inside Container B rises. For every 1 inch (2.5 cm) that Piston A is pushed down, Piston B rises 0.1 inch (one-tenth of an inch or 0.3 cm).

This happens because every pound of force that is placed on Piston A exerts 10 pounds (4.5 kg) of force on Piston B. In other words, if there is a 100-pound (45-kg) weight resting on Piston B, a downward force of only 10 pounds (4.5 kg) is needed to lift it. Of course to raise the 100-pound (45-kg) weight up 1 inch (2.5 cm), you must move piston A a distance of 10 inches (25 cm).

Review of Basic Scientific Principles

ELEMENTS, ATOMS, AND MOLECULES

There are ninety-two naturally occurring *elements* on Earth. An element is a substance made up of many identical *atoms*. An atom is the smallest unit of an element that still has all the properties of the element.

Sometimes an atom combines with other atoms to form a *molecule*. The molecules of elements contain only one type of atom. The molecules of *compounds* contain two or more different types of atoms. There are thousands and thousands of compounds on Earth. Individual molecules are still much too small to see. Any substance that is large enough to see is made of millions of molecules.

GENERAL PROPERTIES OF MATTER

All matter takes up space, and all matter can exist in three forms: solid, liquid, and gas. A solid has a definite volume and shape. Some examples of solids are baseball bats, baseballs, roller skates, frying pans, birthday cakes, and ice cubes. A liquid has definite volume but no definite shape. Examples of liquids are ammonia, orange juice, motor oil, and molasses. A gas has no definite shape and no definite volume. Examples are the exhaust gases of a car, the air we breathe, and the helium gas that fills a balloon.

The form in which matter exists at any given time is determined by its temperature and pressure.

English and Metric Measurements

ENGLISH UNITS OF LENGTH

1 foot = 12 inches
1 yard = 3 feet
1 mile = 1,760 yards
1 mile = 5,280 feet

METRIC UNITS OF LENGTH

1 millimeter (mm) = 1/1,000 meter
1 centimeter (cm) = 1/100 meter
1 decimeter (dm) = 1/10 meter
1 kilometer (km) = 1000 meters

CONVERSION TABLE FOR UNITS OF LENGTH

English to Metric
1 inch = 2.540 centimeters
1 foot = 0.305 meter
1 yard = 0.914 meter
1 mile = 1.609 kilometers

Metric to English
1 centimeter = 0.39 inch
1 meter = 39.37 inches = 3.28 feet = 1.094 yards
1 kilometer = 0.62 mile

ENGLISH UNITS OF AREA

1 square foot = 144 square inches
1 square yard = 9 square feet

METRIC UNITS OF AREA

1 square centimeter (sq cm) = 1/10,000 square meter
1 square decimeter (sq dm) = 1/100 square meter

CONVERSION TABLE FOR UNITS OF AREA

English to Metric
1 square inch = 6.451 square centimeters
1 square foot = 0.093 square meter
1 square yard = 0.835 square meter
1 square mile = 2.588 square kilometers

Metric to English
1 square centimeter = 0.152 square inch
1 square kilometer   = 0.384 square mile

Glossary

atom the smallest unit of an element that still has all the properties of the element.

bale the part of a pulley to which the axle is attached.

block and tackle a compound pulley.

bolt a type of screw that is tightened and loosened with a wrench rather than with a screwdriver.

buoyant capable of floating.

chuck an adjustable drill bit holder.

circumference the distance around the outside of a wheel.

compound a substance made of two or more types of atoms.

elasticity an object's ability to revert to its original shape after being deformed.

element a substance that contains only one type of atom. Examples include pure gold and the neon in a fluorescent sign.

energy a measure of a system's ability to do work.

first-class lever a lever with an input force at one end, an output (or opposing) force at the other end, and a fulcrum in the center.

force a push or a pull.

friction a force that resists the motion between two objects or surfaces. If there is motion and friction is created, energy is converted to heat.

fulcrum the point about which a lever pivots.

gear a type of wheel with teeth.

gravity a force that pulls objects toward the surface of the Earth.

hardness a measure of an object's ability to scratch another object.

helix an object that is shaped like a spiral.

horizontal side to side, flat, straight across, parallel to the horizon.

hydraulic operated by means of a liquid such as water or oil.

inertia a property of matter. An object at rest will stay at rest unless acted upon by an outside force. An object in motion will stay in motion in a straight line unless acted upon by an outside force.

inclined plane a plane surface that is set at an angle.

input force the force exerted on a tool by the person using it.

lever a bar that turns around a pivot point and is used to transfer a force.

lubricant a material that reduces friction.

mass the total amount of matter that makes up an object.

matter everything around us in the universe, except for energy; all solids, liquids, and gases.

mechanical advantage the ratio of the input force (force exerted by you) to the output force (force exerted by the tool you are using). A lever is one type of tool that decreases the amount of input force needed to accomplish work. The greater output force is generated by moving a smaller input force over a greater distance.

mineral a chemical compound that is not living (quartz, diamond, oil, sand, water).

molecule a group of atoms that form the smallest unit of a substance that can exist and retain its chemical properties.

output force the force exerted by a tool.

pressure force per unit area.

second-class lever a lever with the fulcrum at one end, the input force at the other end, and the output (or opposing) force in the center.

sharpness a measure of how fine the edge of an object is.

tempered hardened by the application of heat and subsequent quenching in water or oil.

third-class lever a lever with the fulcrum at one end, the output (or opposing) force at the other end, and the input force in the middle.

torque a force that tends to produce rotation. When you turn on a faucet, the force you exert twists or rotates the handle. This twisting force is torque.

vertical up and down, upright, or perpendicular to the horizon.

volume the amount of space occupied by a three-dimensional object; length multiplied by height.

washer a donut-shaped disk that is inserted between a screw or bolt and the surface of a material. It spreads pressure from the screw or bolt head over a larger area so that the head of the screw or bolt will not be pulled through the material.

weight the measure of the pull of gravity on an object. Since gravity differs on different planets and their satellites such as the moon, the weight of an object can change. The mass of an object is not affected by a change in gravity.

work in physics, work occurs when there is movement caused by the application of a force. Just the fact that energy is expended, however, is not a sign of work. If you were to try to lift a heavy rock, but were unsuccessful, even though you used a great deal of energy and exhausted yourself, you accomplished no work. On the other hand, if you were playing in a school yard and you kicked a soccer ball 10 yards (9 m), you have accomplished work. Your kick applied a force to the soccer ball and the ball moved. The same applies to taking a roller coaster ride. As the car you are in starts to move along the track, work is being accomplished. Accomplishing work can sometimes be fun.

For Further Reading

Better Homes and Gardens Handyman's Book, Des Moines, IA: Better Homes & Gardens, n.d.

Epstein, Lewis Carroll, *Thinking Physics*, San Francisco: Insight Press, 1978.

Grolier Multimedia Encyclopedia, release 6, Danbury, CT: Grolier Electronic Publishing, 1993.

Macauly, David, *The Way Things Work*, Boston: Houghton Mifflin, 1988.

McGraw-Hill Concise Encyclopedia of Science and Technology, New York: McGraw Hill, 1984.

Walker, Jearl, *The Flying Circus of Physics*, New York: Wiley & Sons, 1977.

Index

Numbers in *italics* indicate illustrations.

About the Author

Bob Friedhoffer has a master's degree in liberal studies, with an emphasis on the history and philosophy of science from the City University of New York. Also known as the Madman of Magic, he has been performing as a magician for almost 30 years. Bob frequently lectures on science and magic. His entertaining approach to science can be found in more than a dozen Franklin Watts books.

DEMCO